This Coloring Book Belongs to:

____

____

Dear Bird Enthusiast,

Welcome to the "North American Bird Coloring Book," a vibrant celebration of the avian wonders that grace our continent. Within these pages, you'll discover a kaleidoscope of colors, patterns, and textures waiting to be brought to life by your creativity.

As you embark on this artistic journey, take a moment to marvel at the diversity of birdlife found across North America. From the iconic Bald Eagle to the charming Eastern Bluebird, each species has its own story to tell, its own unique role in our ecosystem.

Whether you're a seasoned birder or a newcomer to the world of birds, this coloring book offers a chance to deepen your connection with nature. With every stroke of your pencil, you'll learn a little more about these fascinating creatures and the habitats they call home.

So, spread your wings and let your imagination soar as you color your way through the pages of this book. May it inspire you to appreciate the beauty of birds and the importance of protecting their habitats for generations to come.

Happy coloring!

Marilyn Glover